A Special Gift
WITH LOVE TO

From

Copyright © 1995 by Christian Art. All rights reserved

Published in South Africa by Christian Art Publishers
P.O. Box 1599, Vereeniging, South Africa

Coedition arranged by Christian Art, South Africa

Design & Photographic Styling: Lizette Jonker

Photography:
Mariam Gillan (cover, floral frames, p 21*, 37#)
Lizette Jonker (p 9, 13, 17, 29, 33, 41, 45)
Julia Lloyd (p 25#)
* Courtesy of *Essentials*
# Courtesy of *Rooi Rose*

Scriptural texts from:
• The Living Bible, Coverdale House Publishers Ltd.
• Special Edition Good News Bible, © Bible Society, London, 1979

ISBN 0-8007-7163-X

Printed in Singapore

WITH LOVE TO ...

Someone Special

Fleming H. Revell
A Division of Baker Book House
Grand Rapids, Michigan 49516

There are four things that are
too mysterious for me to understand:
an eagle flying in the sky, a snake moving
on a rock, a ship finding its way over the sea,
and a man and a woman falling in love.

~ Proverbs 30:18 ~

Drink to me only with thine eyes,
And I will pledge with mine;
Or leave a kiss but in the cup
And I'll not look for wine.

~ Ben Jonson ~

10

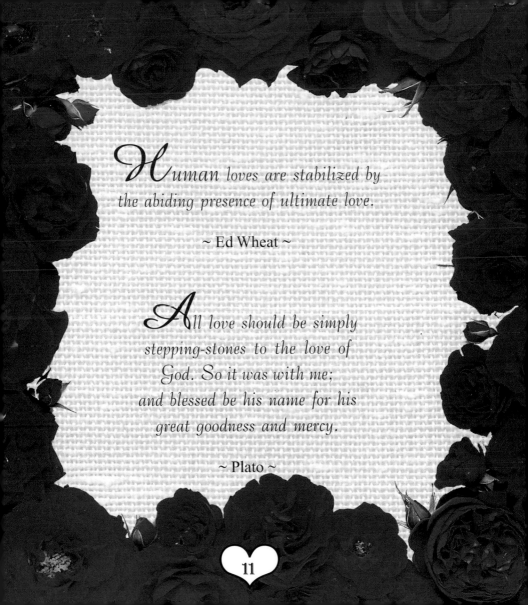

Human loves are stabilized by
the abiding presence of ultimate love.

~ Ed Wheat ~

All love should be simply
stepping-stones to the love of
God. So it was with me;
and blessed be his name for his
great goodness and mercy.

~ Plato ~

11

Love demands all,
and has a right to all.

~ Ludwig von Beethoven ~

One word frees us
of all the weight
and pain of life;
that word is love.

~ Sophocles ~

Close your heart to every love but mine;
hold no one in your arms but me.
Love is as powerful as death;
passion is as strong as death itself.
It bursts into flame
and burns like a raging fire.
Water cannot put it out;
no flood can drown it.

~ Song of Songs 8:6-7 ~

14

*T*he truth about love, I think, is that it is indeed a profound comfort, but it also is a monumental challenge. Love immediately challenges me to break the fixation I have with myself.

~ John Powell ~

*T*his is one of the miracles of love: It gives ... a power of seeing through its own enchantments and yet not being disenchanted.

~ C.S. Lewis ~

Grow old along with me!
The best is yet to be.

~ Robert Browning ~

Of all the earthly music that
reaches farthest into heaven is
the beating of a truly loving heart.

~ Henry Ward Beecher ~

16

*Falling in love is not an extension
of one's limits or boundaries; it is a
partial and temporary collapse of them.*

~ M. Scott Peck ~

*Don't be afraid to let your loyalty be seen.
Tie it around your neck; get it out in the open.
But have it inside as well. Write it on your heart!*

~ William J. Krutza ~

A loving heart is the truest wisdom.

~ Charles Dickens ~

The giving of love is an education in itself.

~ Eleanor Roosevelt ~

*Love does not consist in gazing at each other
but in looking together in the same direction.*

~ Antoine de Saint-Exupéry ~

My lover is like the wild flowers
that bloom in the vineyards at Engedi.

~ Song of Songs 1:14 ~

Love is like a beautiful flower which
I may not touch, but whose fragrance makes
the garden a place of delight just the same.

~ Helen Keller ~

If but one life is transformed
because you lived a life of love,
your contribution to the world will be felt.

~ Reuben Youngdahl ~

*L*ove cannot help loving, any more than
water can help flowing. It is pure joy just to love.

~ Amy Carmichael ~

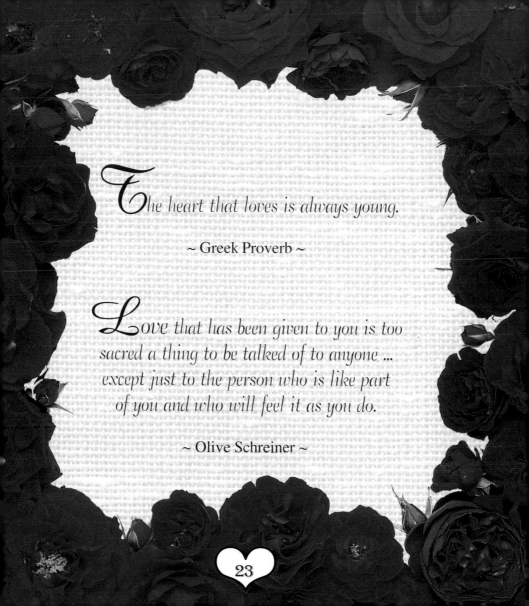

The heart that loves is always young.

~ Greek Proverb ~

Love that has been given to you is too
sacred a thing to be talked of to anyone ...
except just to the person who is like part
of you and who will feel it as you do.

~ Olive Schreiner ~

23

Oh my luve's like a red, red, rose,
That's newly sprung in June:
Oh my luve's like the melodie,
That's sweetly played in tune.

Till a' the seas gang dry, my dear,
And the rocks melt wi' the sun;
And I will luve thee still, my dear,
While the sands o' life shall run.

~ Robert Burns ~

24

Love is patient and kind; it is not jealous or conceited or proud; love is not ill-mannered or selfish or irritable; love does not keep a record of wrongs; love is not happy with evil, but is happy with the truth. Love never gives up; and its faith, hope and patience never fail.

~ 1 Corinthians 13:4-7 ~

When two people have a bond with each other, they share their deepest thoughts, dreams, and feelings with each other with no fear that they will be rejected by the other person.

~ Henry Cloud ~

To love somebody is not just a strong feeling — it is a decision, it is a judgment, it is a promise.

~ Erich Fromm ~

$\mathcal{O}ne$ of the diseases to afflict this century is a loss of wonder. We cannot revere creation if we have lost our wonder about it.

~ Madeleine L'Engle ~

You are always new.
The last of your kisses
was ever the sweetest ...

~ John Keats ~

Love comforteth like sunshine after rain.

~ William Shakespeare ~

In the first chapter boy meets girl. In the last chapter boy kisses girl. The book tells why it took so long.

~ G.K. Chesterton ~

Come then, my love;

my darling, come with me.

The winter is over; the rains have stopped;

in the countryside the flowers are in bloom.

This is the time for singing;

the song of doves is heard in the fields.

Figs are beginning to ripen;

the air is fragrant with blossoming vines.

Come then, my love;

my darling, come with me.

~ Song of Songs 2:10-13 ~

32

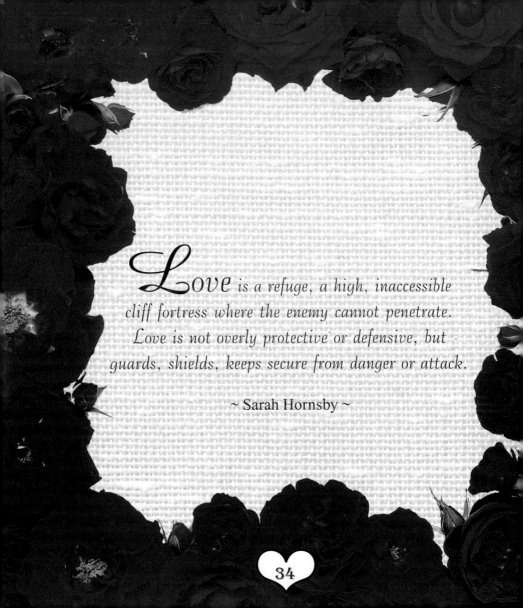

Love is a refuge, a high, inaccessible cliff fortress where the enemy cannot penetrate. Love is not overly protective or defensive, but guards, shields, keeps secure from danger or attack.

~ Sarah Hornsby ~

34

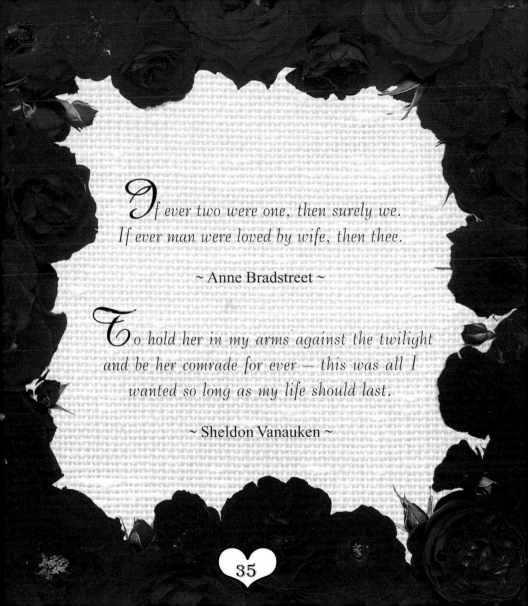

If ever two were one, then surely we.
If ever man were loved by wife, then thee.

~ Anne Bradstreet ~

To hold her in my arms against the twilight
and be her comrade for ever — this was all I
wanted so long as my life should last.

~ Sheldon Vanauken ~

Nevertheless, I am in a dream, a flustered, happy, hurried dream. I can't believe that it is going to be; and yet I can't believe but that every one I pass in the street, must have some kind of perception, that I am to be married the day after tomorrow.

~ Charles Dickens ~

No love, no friendship can
cross the path of our destiny without
leaving some mark on it forever.

~ François Mauriac ~

Love cures people, the ones who
receive love and the ones who give it.

~ Karl A. Menninger ~

38

*B*rief is life but long is love.

~ Alfred, Lord Tennyson ~

*H*appiness seems made to be shared.

~ Jean Racine ~

My sweetheart, my bride, is a secret garden,
a walled garden, a private spring;
there the plants flourish.

They grow like an orchard of pomegranate-
trees and bear the finest fruits.

There is no lack of henna and nard,
of saffron, calamus, and cinnamon,
or incense of every kind.
Myrrh and aloes grow there
with all the most fragrant perfumes.

Fountains water the garden,
streams of flowing water,
brooks gushing down from the Lebanon Mountains.

~ Song of Songs 4:12-15 ~

40

So long as we love we serve, so long as we are loved by others, I would almost say that we are indispensable.

~ Robert Louis Stevenson ~

The happiness of life is made up of minute fractions – the little soon-forgotten charities of a kiss or a smile, a kind look, or heartfelt compliment.

~ Samuel Taylor Coleridge ~

Kind words can be short and easy to speak, but their echoes are truly endless.

~ Mother Teresa ~

Unshared joy is an unlighted candle.

~ Spanish Proverb ~

*Of all earthly music, that which reaches farthest
into heaven is the beating of a truly loving heart.*

~ Henry Ward Beecher ~